TIPS AND TRICKS TO OPTIMIZE YOUR DIRECT RESPONSE MARKETING

Written by

EMERY V. BROWN

TABLE OF CONTENTS

DIRECT RESPONSE MARKETING EXPLAINED

Direct response marketing is a strategy that elicits an immediate response from your target audience. The desired response isn't always a sale. It could be signing up for a newsletter, reading a blog post, or taking advantage of a lead magnet.

Many people associate direct response marketing with direct mail, but it works equally as well with:

- Social media ads
- PPC ads
- Landing pages
- Email
- Traditional media

Direct response marketing is designed to generate immediate results, which nets you an immediate return on your investment.

The advantage of direct response marketing is that you can get real-time data about what's working and what's not so that you can always get optimal results.

But, what does it take to be successful with direct response marketing? There are some key components that you can implement to ensure that you get the results you want from your marketing campaigns.

HAVE A UNIQUE SELLING PROPOSITION

Your unique selling proposition is the thing that makes your business different from everyone else in your market. It's the thing that makes YOU stand out and the reason the customer should buy from YOU.

Identifying a USP may be easier for some businesses than others, depending on what the business is and how much competition there is in the market.

Fortunately, you can carve out a name for yourself even if you make or sell a fairly common product or service.

Having a strong USP can focus your marketing strategy and influence your messaging, branding, copywriting, and marketing decisions.

WHAT MAKES A STRONG USP?

A strong USP generally addresses a specific need being experienced by the ideal customer. Customers can be overwhelmed with options when it comes to making a purchase. They want to quickly know what makes one product/ service better than the rest.

Knowing how to position your products and services the right way can make the difference between standing out and getting lost in the crowd.

Your USP should highlight your strengths and be based on what makes your product or service valuable to your ideal customer.

A compelling USP will be:

- **Focused on what your ideal customer values.** Just being unique isn't going to cut it. Find something you offer that your customers truly care about.

- **Defensively assertive.** Take a position that forces you to make a case for your products and against the competition. Everyone says their products are *the best* or *high quality.* What makes yours stand out?

- **Not just a slogan.** Slogans are fun and have their place in your branding message but your USP embodies who you are as a company.

A great USP is an intersection between what your customers want and what your business does well.

GET INTO YOUR PERFECT CUSTOMER'S HEAD

Before you start trying to figure out what sets your business apart from your competition, you need to really get into the head of your perfect customer. Be sure you know who your perfect customer actually is - the real nitty-gritty of who is actually going to want to buy your product.

Don't just settle for targeting a rough demographic of who you think will buy your product. Push yourself to identify exactly who you want to sell to and why.

Once you know who that is, consider these questions:

- How does your product/service solve their problems?
- What motivates their buying decisions?
- Why do your existing customers choose your product/service over the competition?
- What does your ideal customer really want?

HOW DOES YOUR PRODUCT/SERVICE SOLVE YOUR TARGET CUSTOMERS PROBLEMS?

Most customers don't just want to buy products, they want to solve problems - their problems. This is why it's imperative that you know your target audience so well. In order to create an effective USP, you have to know the profile of your customer so you can market your products in a way that shows them you can solve their problems and meet their needs.

If you don't know the voice of your customer, it will be difficult for you to write compelling, persuasive copy. Be prepared to **show them how your product will:**

- Improve their life
- Make them choose you over the competition

Once you know exactly who your customer is and what problems they're dealing with, it's time to tell them exactly why they should choose you over the competition.

WHAT A USP IS NOT

A unique selling proposition is not a slogan or tagline. It's also not a specific marketing offer. Free shipping, 24/7 customer service, and 15% off your first order are not USPs.

While these strategies may work to make sales and garner some customers, they are not unique or defensible because your competition can use the exact same ploys. **Your USP should be unique - something they can only get from you.**

A USP is an assertion that distinguishes your brand and products from your competition. It's a position your business takes that can be woven into your brand, products, and the experience you provide to the customer.

HOW TO WRITE A UNIQUE SELLING PROPOSITION FOR YOUR BUSINESS

This may seem like an overwhelming task, especially if you're just getting started in business, but it's well worth the time because everything (your brand, marketing, etc.) will flow from it.

1. List your differentiating qualities.

Your USP should not be interchangeable with another business. It should be unique to *your* business and your product/service.

Be really specific about how you're different from your competition. A compelling marketing message relies on precision. It solves the exact problems the customer has and communicates the benefits.

2. Stalk the competition.

What are your competitor's USPs? Look for ways that you can market your product differently. Just because your products are in the same general category doesn't mean they can't be positioned in different ways.

Try making a list of your competitors and evaluate how they are meeting the customer's needs. **Even if they have a desirable position in the market, they may not be delivering on their promises.** Being able to do it better is a strong basis for entering the market.

Find any pain points that haven't been met already by the competition. These are the places where you can appeal to the customers.

3. Make your USP rich in hyperbole.

Many businesses are hesitant to use hyperbole because it seems sales-y or arrogant, but it really can be helpful in this situation. Don't say you *make comfortable slippers* - say you *make the world's most comfortable slippers.*

Use words like *best, greatest, first, favorite, demand, only, etc.* **Consider these examples of great USPs:**

- Death Wish Coffee Co. - **The World's Strongest Coffee**
- Thrive Market - **Belong to a better market**
- Third Love - **We have the right fit**
- Saddleback Leather - **They'll fight over it when you're dead**

4. Always focus on the benefit to the customer, not the actual product or service.

Remember, you're giving the customer a post-sales environment. Your USP should be about the world they can enjoy or the reality they can have after they purchase.

Your ideal customer doesn't really care about the product. **What they really care about is not having to deal with their current problem anymore.** This is what your USP should convey.

Sell the feeling. Look at the marketing for any fragrance brand. They don't talk about the product, they show you what life is like when you use the product. Beautiful, seductive, sassy, romantic - this is how life will be after you use this product.

OFFER A LEAD MAGNET

A lead magnet is something that is given away in exchange for a person's contact information. Lead magnets are used to generate leads, and odds are you've signed up with your email address to get one.

Think about a time you were on a website and they offered a free ebook, a trial subscription to a service, or a white paper. All you had to do was give up your email address right? The lead magnet was undoubtedly delivered right to your inbox.

The reason lead magnets are so essential to your direct response program is that they create warm leads along with a way to get in touch with them *directly*.

WHAT SHOULD YOU OFFER?

Your lead magnet doesn't necessarily have to be directly related to your product or service. **It does, however, need to be something that someone who's interested in your product or service would be willing to give up their email address for.** It has to be something valuable since people protect their email from possible spam very diligently.

For example, if you're selling a product or service related to healthy living, you could give away an ebook about the importance of gut health. People who are interested in healthy living are generally concerned about their gut health.

There are many options when it comes to the form your lead magnet takes. You can create an e-course or an ebook, both of which are very popular options but do require a bit of time and investment on your part.

Infographics and articles are also quite popular. If you're more of a service-based business, consider offering a free consultation.

Whatever you decide to offer, the important thing is that someone interested in your product would want that information. When you give your website visitors something useful for free (the cost of their email address) and the information is useful, they will trust you. You become an expert in their eyes and who they will turn to when they are ready to purchase.

Here are some top-notch ideas for lead magnet offers:

- E-book
- Online course
- Infographic
- Article

- Free newsletter
- Quiz
- How-to guide
- Checklist
- Online events

The lead magnet that you provide your customers will be dependent on the product or service that you provide.

THE CONVERSION PATH

So, what's the right way to offer a lead magnet? The first thing you need is traffic coming to your website, which you can get through SEO, blog posts, paid ads, social media, etc.

Regardless of how you get your traffic, the conversion path is pretty much the same:

- **Call-to-action.** This tells the visitor where to go to get the resource you're offering. It's generally a button that they can push to get access. You can also design a slide-in or pop up with your magnet offer.

- **Landing page.** This is where the customer's information is captured. It's usually a form that collects the customer's name, email address, and any other information pertinent to your lead magnet or future marketing plans.

- **Thank-you page.** Once the customer has filled out the form, they should be directed to a thank you page where you thank them and let them know how to access the magnet.

- **Form submission kickback email.** Once they've signed up, there should be an automated email that goes out immediately to their email address, thanking them again for signing up and giving them information about how to access the resource you've provided.

Once you have their email address, you can begin an email marketing campaign or keep them updated about your products and services.

DESIGN AN AUTOMATED, SEQUENTIAL, FOLLOW-UP EMAIL CAMPAIGN

Lead magnets, email opt-ins, and landing pages will attract new subscribers, but building a relationship requires the right email sequences.

An email sequence is pre-written, pre-scheduled emails sent to your subscribers. It may provide educational information, product information, current promotions, or what the next step is.

Because the emails provide ongoing education, information, and exposure to your product or service; your audience is primed to purchase from you.

Before pitching your offer, it's a good idea to build trust with the subscriber. Email campaigns are about building trust. Your subscribers want to feel like you understand their pain points, see where they're struggling, and that you're passionate about helping them resolve their problems.

Once you fulfill these needs, your email subscriber is well on their way to making a purchase from you.

TYPES OF EMAIL SEQUENCES

Email sequences are a great way to engage with your existing customers and new subscribers. They allow you to provide them with helpful information and also provide you with easy upsell opportunities to increase their lifetime customer value.

You can create sequences for all kinds of reasons - welcome sequences, lead magnet sequences, etc. And your sequences can also be specific to the type of business that you have.

Let's take a look at some popular email sequences you can implement in your business.

1. Welcome sequence.

Almost 75% of emails subscribers expect to get a welcome email from you, so don't disappoint them! It's important to take a minute to introduce yourself, explain what you have to offer, and how your offer is relevant to *them.*

Just one email may not be enough - you want to nurture your new subscribers after all. The welcome sequence is less about making money for you and more about building a relationship with your subscribers. Use this time to share stories with your subscribers and build trust.

If you are a coach or freelancer, use this time to talk about your philosophy on success and thought leadership. If you're an educator, you can share information about your expertise and give tips subscribers can implement for whatever they're learning.
A blogger can share their favorite or most relevant blog posts.

Showing a more personal side through your welcome sequence builds a stronger connection with the subscriber.

Plan out your welcome sequence by making a list of stories, tips, blog posts, etc., that you'd like to share. From there you can determine how you'd like the content to flow throughout your sequence.

Remember to always point your writing back to the audience and how it relates to them.

2. Onboarding email sequence.

An onboarding email sequence should start once someone makes a purchase from you. Think of it as a list of instructions or helpful advice for your new customer, just with more personality.

An onboarding sequence can help them understand how to effectively use the product. You can even offer tips on how to implement the product into their daily lives.

If you sell a service, consider starting the onboarding sequence when the client books the first appointment. Use this email sequence to set boundaries and expectations for the client.

Onboarding email sequences can be very flexible, and whether you have a physical product or you're providing a service, you can definitely find a way to make them fit your needs. They are an automated tool for you to equip your audience with more information and build your relationship with them further.

3. Abandoned cart sequence.

This type of email sequence can help you re-engage with a customer who left a product in their shopping cart without making a purchase.

Studies show that up to 75% of shopping carts are abandoned before making the purchase. **An email sequence can help boost conversions by reminding the customer what made them put the item into their cart in the first place.**

Creating an automated sequence gives you the chance to keep engaging the customer and increase the likelihood that they will come back and convert that empty cart into a sale.

An abandoned cart sequence might look something like this:

- The **first email** should be a light-hearted reminder that they have an item left in their cart.

- If they open that email, but **still don't make the purchase** it will trigger another email offering a discount or more information to earn more trust.

You may be wondering if abandoned cart sequences actually work and if they're worth the trouble. The answer is YES.

Over 45% of subscribers open abandoned cart emails. About 14% click on the call to action within the email, and of those that click, 35% will actually complete the purchase.

When a customer puts an item in their cart, they are engaging with your brand, which means they have a strong interest in what you're selling. Don't miss out on getting this conversion.

4. Event email sequence.

If you're hosting an event (whether online or in-person) such as a workshop or conference, there are two types of email sequences you'll want to send. One is for the people who haven't signed up yet, and the other is for the people who have already reserved their spot.

The first sequence will be sent to your entire list of subscribers. In the email you can highlight:

- Event details
- Attendee benefits
- Success stories from your last event
- The offer for your current event

The second sequence goes out to the customers who have already purchased their ticket. In this sequence you can:

- Provide more details
- Answer frequently asked questions
- Let them know what they should bring

Being able to send this second sequence will save you so much time fielding questions from ticket holders before the event. You can simply direct them to the emails being sent to them.

5. Re-engagement email sequence.

This sequence is directed at your cold subscribers.

Cold subscribers are defined as people who have been on your list for more than 30 days but have not opened an email from you in at least 90 days.

Continuing to email a list of cold subscribers who never engage with your emails is not a good marketing strategy. Not only are you paying to send them the emails that will never be opened, your open and click rates will be skewed. In turn, you may make marketing decisions based on bad information, which could end up hurting your marketing campaigns in the long run.

To re-engage cold subscribers, send an email sequence that starts with a potential breakup message.

In the email, let them know that you're potentially going to remove them from your email list if they don't engage in some way. Then invite them to re-join your email list.

BEST PRACTICES WHEN CREATING AN AUTOMATED EMAIL SEQUENCE

If you're just getting started with automated email sequences, don't try to do all of them at once. Start out with just one area that you'd like to work on. Every email sequence you create gives you more data and experience you can use to make future decisions.

Here are some good places to start based on the type of product/service you provide:

- If you **create a product**, a great place to start is with an abandoned cart sequence. This can help boost your conversions right away.

- If you **create content**, consider creating a welcome sequence to follow up with your new subscribers after they have accepted your lead magnet. You can continue building connections to your new subscribers through your email sequence.

- **Freelancers or service providers** may choose to start with an onboarding sequence. It will save so much time and allow you to refocus on serving your clients.

The style and format of your emails are important, but it's most important that you keep them simple. If your email takes forever to load, your subscriber will delete it without reading it. So, don't load them up with images - stick to plain text as much as possible.

STAND OUT SUBJECT LINES

Stand-out subject lines are everything. This is what the subscriber sees that makes them decide whether they're going to spend their time opening your email.

You can have the greatest email in the history of marketing, but if your headline is flat it won't get opened.

USE RELEVANT IMAGES AND VIDEOS TO ENGAGE YOUR AUDIENCE

Visual content, like images and videos, is a smart way to bring in more traffic and engage your audience. Videos, photos, and graphics grab the user's attention much faster than text.

SCIENTIFIC FACTS AND STATISTICS ABOUT VISUAL CONTENT

There are scientific reasons why visual content is so important to include when engaging your audience:

- It takes about 60 seconds to read 200-250 words, while it only takes about 1/10 of a second for our brains to understand a photo.

- Visual information is retained 6x more than information read or heard.

- Websites with images have about 47% more click-through rates.

- Infographics get 12% more traffic to a site and 200% more shares on social media.

- Content with relevant images gets 94% more views than those without.

- Video generates 80% more conversions than content without videos.

It's well worth the time and energy to include images and videos in your content. People are bombarded with data all day long and it's nice to get a break from that with a photo or video.

STRATEGIES FOR USING VISUAL CONTENT

About 90% of the brain's daily data processing is done through visual means. Visuals are consumed 40% more effectively and 60,000x faster than text. Our brains are amazing.

Keep these strategies in mind when using videos and imagery:

1. Choose relevant, authentic images. Stock images are great and readily available, but they aren't always exactly relevant. Make sure your images add value to your content and convey the message you're trying to get across. Images and videos can be amazing storytellers if used correctly.

2. Use a variety of visuals. Always try to think of how you can visually present your content or how you can support your content in an authentic way through images.

- Try using infographics if you're presenting a lot of data or statistics.
- Include pictures of the products you mention.
- Use photos in your tutorials to illustrate the process you're explaining.

3. Don't share copyrighted images. Using someone else's images should not be done as it can result in costly legal trouble. A good rule of thumb is if you made it, it's safe to use. If you found it on someone else's site, you need a license or written permission to use it.

4. Optimize for SEO. Always optimize your images for SEO. Search engine tech has come a long way, and with about 27% of all searches being for images, it's well worth the bump you'll get in traffic.

Be sure to include an image description with keywords and be specific when describing the image. Also, add an ALT tag with keywords for better indexing.

5. Add social media buttons to your images. People are more likely to share images than text, so make it easy for them. This is such a simple thing you can do to drive more traffic to your site.

Using images and videos can easily help drive more traffic to your site.

OPTIMIZE YOUR SITE TO BE MOBILE FRIENDLY

If you've ever visited a website from your mobile device, you know how frustrating it can be if that site has not been optimized for mobile use. Endless scrolling, photos that don't load, and tiny buttons and links have users running for the hills.

The more frustrated a customer becomes, the less likely they are to convert, or even stay on the page. They'll be long gone and won't look back.

HOW MOBILE OPTIMIZATION AFFECTS CONVERSIONS

Mobile optimization increases conversions by reducing the frustrations of your audience.

More than ever, people are using their smartphones to access websites. In fact, users spend about twice as much time accessing the web on their mobile devices than their laptops or desktops. This is why optimization is essential for online businesses.

A mobile-friendly website facilitates more conversions by including the following features:

- Larger buttons
- Autofill form fields
- Smaller images
- Less scrolling

Less frustration for the consumer means more conversions for you.

TIPS FOR OPTIMIZING YOUR WEBSITE

Now that you know why you should optimize your website, it's time to learn how. Here are some tips on optimizing your website for the best possible results.

1. Choose a responsive web design.

Right out of the gate, choose a web design that is 100% responsive. This means that it conforms to the screen size on which it's viewed. The images become smaller and menu bars are replaced with space-saving *hamburger* menus.

Responsive design is different from mobile optimization. Mobile optimization starts with a responsive design but also creates a completely mobile-ready site. Mobile optimized sites look much different than a responsive site when viewed on a mobile device. It's completely configured with the mobile user in mind.

Using a responsive web design will start you in the right direction and your site will be much more navigable for your visitors, which will improve your conversions.

2. Use structured data.

Structured data is what allows search engines to display rich snippets. These are a part of the Schema markup (HTML code) and add more information for search engines to index. Rich snippets often appear in organic search results.

Using structured data can help Google to rank you more accurately on the search engine results page.

3. Compress your images.

Large image files can cause slower loading pages which will cause your visitors to bounce back to the results page for other options.

Responsive design resizes your images, but an alternative for mobile optimization would be to upload a smaller image file. The image should be large enough to be seen clearly but small enough to not impact your loading speeds.

4. Remove features that are not mobile-friendly.

There are some elements on your website that just might not convert well to a mobile optimized site. Sidebars for example, usually create a situation where the user is pinching the screen to try to read the main text of the page because the sidebar is taking up all of the space.

Remove the clutter and make everything clean and easy to read on your mobile site. This includes flash elements which tend to bog everything down.

5. Use AMP.

Accelerated Mobile Pages (AMP) are mobile-optimized versions of websites. It changes the functionality and looks of your website when it's viewed on a mobile device

AMP websites load much faster than standard websites because it brings up a cached version of the website. Faster load times equals people who stay on your site.

6. Pay special attention to your checkout page.

Cart abandonment is higher on mobile sites than on standard sites simply because the user gets frustrated by slow loading speeds and hard-to-navigate screens. Be sure to get your checkout page optimized for the best possible conversions.

USE SOCIAL MEDIA AND OFFLINE MARKETING TO DRIVE TRAFFIC TO YOUR SITE

The name of the game for any marketing strategy is driving traffic to your site. Without traffic, there can't be conversions, and if there are no conversions, there's no income.

USING SOCIAL MEDIA TO DRIVE TRAFFIC

Social media is a great tool for businesses to use to drive traffic to their websites. After all, social media has billions of users worldwide and more are joining every day. If you use it right, social media can be an effective and affordable way to spread the word about your brand, business, and products.

In order to get the best results from your social media efforts, there are certain actions you have to take.

1. Post content regularly and interact with your followers consistently.

As with everything online, there are algorithms in play. In order to get maximum results, you must post regularly and interact with your followers. This means responding to and liking their comments. Keep in mind that you don't have to post a blog post several times a day. You can mix it up with memes, infographics, and photos. Just be consistent.

Social media followers love to feel like they are involved in a community and if you are responding to their comments, they will be more likely to keep commenting which will help your visibility.

2. Make your content easy to share.

Include social media sharing buttons directly on your content so that your visitors can easily share it on their social media.

3. Post when your audience is most active.

The more interaction your posts get, the more visible your content will be and the more visible your content is, the more traffic you'll get. Try to figure out when your audience is the most active on social media to get the most engagement.

Remember, social media is constantly changing its algorithms. **In order to stay ahead of the game, you want to have as many people engaging with your posts as possible.**

4. Use better calls-to-action.

If you're not seeing the kind of engagement you are hoping for from your social media posts, it may be because you haven't told the reader what you want them to do next. Writing a clear call to action tells the reader what they need to do next and how you want them to interact with your post.

Your goal should be to persuade the reader to click on the link and visit your site. Try testing different phrases to see what gets the best engagement.

OFFLINE MARKETING

Online marketing has taken all of the attention from offline direct response marketing in recent years. However, even offline marketing methods can drive traffic to your site. Here are a few to try:

- Distribute your business cards
- Donate gift certificates or products as contest prizes
- Speak at events relevant to your niche

- Pitch a press release to local media
- Make cold calls
- Participate in trade shows
- Sponsor a community event
- Send out mailers
- Produce a radio ad

GIVE DIRECT RESPONSE MARKETING A TRY

Direct response marketing is a great way to get those conversions up quickly. Using these tips, you can have great success.